Solve-the-Problem Mini-Books

MULTIPLICATION & DIVISION

12 Math Stories for Real-World Problem Solving

by Nancy Belkov

Editor: Pari Deshpande Cohen
Cover design: Mina Chen
Interior design: Grafica Inc.
Illustrations: Steliyana Doneva

ISBN: 978-1-338-80458-4
Scholastic Inc., 557 Broadway, New York, NY 10012
Copyright © 2023 by Nancy Belkov
Published by Scholastic Inc. All rights reserved.
Printed in the U.S.A.
First printing, January 2023.

1 2 3 4 5 6 7 8 9 10   40   32 31 30 29 28 27 26 25 24 23

Table of Contents

Introduction:
Why Use Stories at Math Time?

Stories help us make important connections in our lives. Through the engaging, relatable stories in *Solve-the-Problem Mini-Books*, students can connect with characters as they figure out how to solve math problems. The characters model asking questions, taking risks, identifying mistakes and misconceptions, justifying their thinking, and trying out ideas. By observing these characters, students can discover processes that will help them make sense of math concepts and solve problems thoughtfully.

Making sense of problems and persevering in solving them is vital to students' success. This key math standard is the backbone of this book. Research shows the effectiveness of teaching math concepts through problem solving.[1] To employ this approach, challenge students with unfamiliar problems that are within their grasp without telling them how to find an answer. Instead of mandating use of a specific operation or strategy, encourage students to try a variety of approaches and strategies independently. Guide them to apply prior knowledge to find these solution paths. As students work together to share ideas and strategies, provide them with prompts, questions, ideas, and materials to support their learning. This approach helps students develop confidence and make connections among math concepts.

Learning problem-solving skills takes time. Just as reading regularly helps students become better readers, seeing and doing math regularly helps them understand and become more confident with math. Embed problem solving in relatable contextual situations to help students see math around them and apply new skills in daily life. Use the stories in this book to help make the connection between problem solving and concept learning more symbiotic and to help students develop as problem solvers.

What's in This Book?

In this book you'll find 12 mini-books and companion practice pages that focus primarily on multiplication and division concepts and skills. These give students a problem-solving model and opportunities to apply the representations and strategies demonstrated by the characters.

Each mini-book presents a contextual problem, focusing on one of the different types of problems identified by Carpenter, Fennema, Franke, Levi, and Empson.[2] These include finding an unknown product, an unknown group size, and an unknown number of groups through multiplication and division. Many students struggle to understand these kinds of problems, so exposure to all problem types is important.

---

[1] National Council of Teachers of Mathematics (NCTM). (2010, April 8). *Why Is Teaching With Problem Solving Important to Student Learning?* [Research Brief]

[2] Carpenter, T. P., Fennema, E., Franke, M. L., Levi, L., & Empson, S. B. (2014). *Children's Mathematics*, Second Edition: Cognitively Guided Instruction (2nd ed.). Heinemann.

How to Use the Mini-Books

Integrating these materials into your current math curriculum is easy. As you plan lessons, consider whether your students have prior knowledge that will enable them to relate to new strategies and concepts in the stories. If you use a curriculum in which students already engage with the problem structures in this book, you may want to use the materials selectively, revisiting problem-solving situations with which your students struggle. A chart of the problem-solving strategies modeled in each mini-book is provided as part of the answer key at the back of the book.

Each mini-book begins with a situational math problem that the student characters must solve. This is followed by "Think" questions, which are designed to help your students learn to read a problem many times (three times is often optimal) to make sense of three essentials:

1) the situation of the problem
2) the question the problem is asking
3) the important information students need to answer the question

Taking time to answer these fundamental questions helps students learn processes for making sense of math problems throughout their work as problem solvers and should become an automatic part of their problem solving.

Create the mini-book. Make double-sided copies of the mini-book so that page 2 appears directly behind the title page. Stack the pages in order and staple along the left side. See diagram.

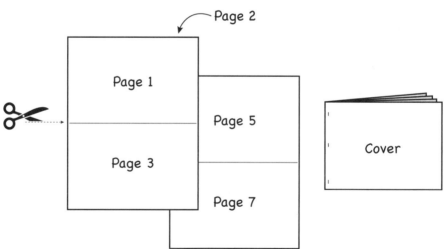

Introduce the mini-book. Students often learn best from other children, so you might introduce a story by saying something like: *Let's see how other students have been solving problems similar to the ones we've been working on.* Project the problem (mini-book page 1) while covering the "Think" questions. Read the problem aloud.

Understand the situation. Uncover the first "Think" question. Successful problem solvers employ a variety of techniques for understanding the problem, including rereading, visualizing, or retelling. Encourage students to try one of the following ways to understand the situation:

- Turn to a partner and describe the situation to each other.
- Draw a picture or diagram to illustrate the situation.
- Act out the situation.

Flexibility with a variety of strategies can help students make sense of problems. Students may use several techniques together or find that one is enough. Facilitate a class share to clarify what is happening in the problem.

Restate the question. Distribute copies of the mini-book. Focusing only on the first page, have students reread the problem and then restate the question in their own words.

Identify the important information. Ask students to identify the information they will need to solve the problem. Discuss why this information is important. Give students the opportunity to think about different ways to use the information, prior knowledge, and modeling tools that might help them solve the problem.

Solve the problem. Students are now ready to think about solution strategies. With some mini-books, you may want students to work in pairs or independently to come up with possible solutions before reading the rest of the story. With others, you may decide to have students move directly to observing how the characters in the story work to solve the problem.

As students read the rest of the story, they will need to process the concepts and strategies the characters use. Whether you use the story as a read-aloud or independent reading, be sure to provide time for discussion and retelling. Encourage students to stop along the way to describe the work the characters do, discuss questions that arise, and try out strategies for themselves. Prompt students to observe how the characters collaborate to solve unfamiliar problems, try out different concepts and strategies, model problems, and reason.

Reflect on the strategies. The last page of each mini-book has "Your Turn" questions to help students analyze the strategies the characters used. These questions provide an opportunity for students to internalize the approaches modeled and clarify underlying math concepts.

Apply the strategies. Finally, use the practice pages to give students the opportunity to try the strategies. These problems encourage students to use at least two problem-solving strategies for each scenario. This promotes self-checking, helps students draw connections, and adds to their toolkits. Have students work independently or in pairs, followed by a class share to address concepts, questions, or struggles.

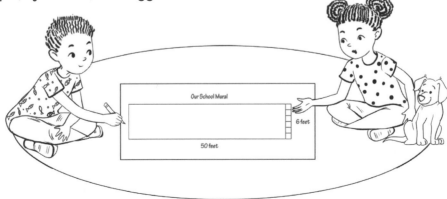

Writing Story Problems

Ms. Thompson asked her students to write and solve story problems for the division sentence 24 ÷ 4 = __. Students split up into pairs to get started.

Think

- What is happening in this story?

- What do the students need to figure out?

- What is the important information?

1

"Will this work for division? *Bob has 4 bags of erasers. Each bag has 24 erasers. How many erasers does Bob have?*" asked Dan.

"That's not division. It's multiplying or adding. You have 4 groups of 24 things. It's 24 + 24 + 24 + 24 or 4 × 24," said Amber.

24 erasers	24 erasers	24 erasers	24 erasers

"You're right. Do you have a story about 24 ÷ 4?" asked Dan.

3

"The problem says we need to divide. What does Ms. Thompson mean when she says write a story problem?" Dan asked Amber.

"She wants us to think about situations when we need to divide 24 by 4. Like a story problem for 20 + 30 could be: *How many books do we have if we started with 20 books and we bought 30 more?*" said Amber.

 2

"Think about putting 24 things into equal groups, like this: *Let's say I have a page of 24 stickers. There are 4 stickers in each row. How many rows of stickers are on the page?*" said Amber.

"I see. You would divide stickers into groups of 4. Can we divide them into 4 groups instead, like this: *I have 24 stickers in 4 equal rows. How many stickers are in each row?*" asked Dan.

"Your problem works, too. Let's put tiles in rows to find the answers. Pretend each tile is one sticker. We can start with 1 row of 4 stickers or 4 rows each with 1 sticker," said Amber.

4

Amber's problem

□ □ □ □

Dan's problem

□
□
□
□

Solve-the-Problem Mini-Books: Multiplication & Division © Nancy Belkov, Scholastic Inc. (page 8)

Dan:
4 rows of stickers

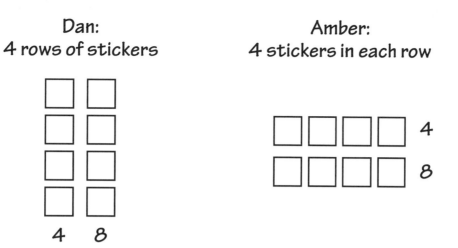

4   8

Amber:
4 stickers in each row

4
8

"I'll finish the 4 rows to see how many stickers would be in each row," said Dan.

"Okay. I'll figure out how many rows we need. Let's skip count as we go. I think we'll get the same number each way," said Amber.

"Now I have a division problem about erasers: *Bob had 24 erasers. He had 4 bags. He put the same number of erasers in each bag. How many erasers did he put in each bag?*" said Dan. "Thanks for helping me figure out how to write a division story problem."

Dan

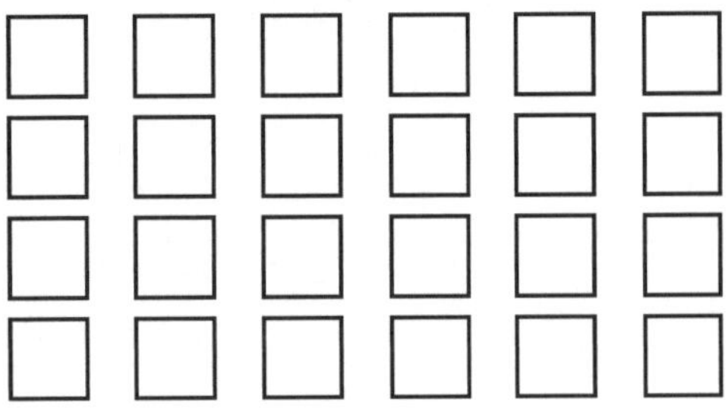

Amber

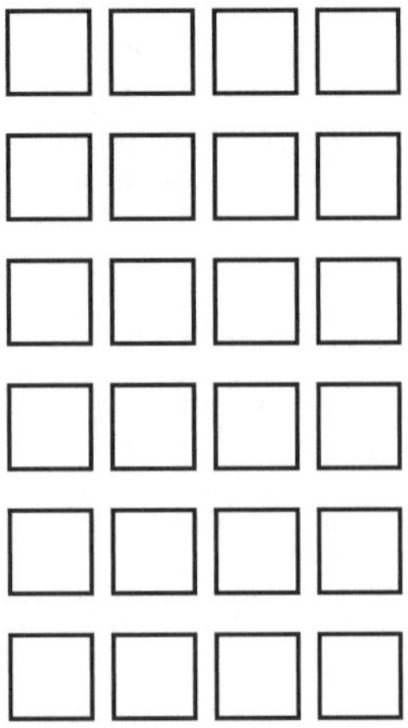

"You made 4 rows, and each row has 6 stickers. So $24 \div 4 = 6$," said Amber. "I put 4 stickers in each row and made 6 rows. That's also $24 \div 4 = 6$."

"I have 4 rows of 6, and you have 6 rows of 4. So $4 \times 6 = 6 \times 4$," observed Dan.

6

Your Turn

• How did Amber and Dan figure out how to write story problems for $24 \div 4$?

• Why do Amber and Dan think that $4 \times 6 = 6 \times 4$?

8

Name: _____

Writing Word Problems

Now you can write some more problems to solve. Amber and Dan thought about what happens with groups in multiplication and in division. See if thinking about putting things in groups or putting groups together helps you write problems of your own. Using facts you know can help you solve the problems. Share your problems with a partner to solve.

1. Write a story problem for the multiplication sentence $5 \times 8 =$ ___.
Solve your problem.

2. Write a story problem for the division sentence $48 \div 6 =$ ____. Solve your problem.

3. Andy wanted to write a story problem for the equation $28 \div 4 =$ ___.

He started the problem by writing,

"My sister had 28 seashells. She took 4 of them and put them in a bag."

Then he was stuck. Help Andy finish his problem about shells. Make any changes you need to make.

4. Ms. Thompson asked Shira to write a story problem for the equation ____ $= 5 \times 9$. She wondered if that equation was the same as $5 \times 9 =$ ____. She decided it must be. She wrote the following:

"My brother had 5 fish in one fishbowl and 9 fish in another."

Then she was stuck. Help Shira write a multiplication story problem about fish in fishbowls for the equation $5 \times 9 =$ ____.

Extension: Change the numbers in one of the problems above or create your own problem about dividing things into a certain number of groups. Solve your problem.

Solve-the-Problem Mini-Books: Multiplication & Division © Nancy Belkov, Scholastic Inc. (page 12)

Greeting Cards

David and Lucia made 48 greeting cards to sell at a school fundraiser. They will sell them in sets of 6 cards and need 1 bag to hold each set. Ms. Thompson asked them how many bags they will need.

Solve-the-Problem Mini-Books: Multiplication & Division © Nancy Belkov, Scholastic Inc.

Think

- What is happening in this story?

- What do the students need to figure out?

- What is the important information?

1

"So far, I have 2 bags with 6 cards in each bag. I'll make another bag with 6 in it, to keep dividing our 48 cards into sets," said Lucia.

"Then you will have 6 + 6 + 6. I know that 3 × 6 = 18. Let's use that multiplication fact to divide our cards into bags," said David.

"But we are dividing, not multiplying," said Lucia.

Solve-the-Problem Mini-Books: Multiplication & Division © Nancy Belkov, Scholastic Inc. (page 13)

3

"I don't know how many bags we need yet. Let's just start decorating bags and see what we need," David said to Lucia.

"But Ms. Thompson wants to give us only the number of bags that we need. Let's draw 6 cards in a bag. Then repeat that to see how many bags we need for 48 cards," said Lucia.

Lucia drew a rectangle for a bag and drew 6 sticks in it for the cards. David said he could just write the number 6 on the next bag.

"Yes, but multiplication helps us with division. We know that $3 \times 6 = 18$, so $18 \div 6 = 3$. We can divide up 18 cards into sets of 6 for our first 3 bags. Then we can use 18 more cards and make 3 more bags of 6 cards. That's 36 cards in bags," said David.

6 cards	6 cards	6 cards

$3 \times 6 = 18$

$18 + 18 = 36$

6 cards	6 cards	6 cards

$3 \times 6 = 18$

| 6 cards | 6 cards | $2 \times 6 = 12$ | We need
3 bags + 3 bags + 2 bags |

"Let's finish putting the 48 cards in bags. We still have 12 cards because $48 - 36 = 12$," said David.

"I know that $12 \div 6 = 2$ since $2 \times 6 = 12$. So we need 2 more bags. The 3 bags we just made + 3 bags that we already had, and then 2 more bags. Now we have 8 bags total. $8 \times 6 = 48$ so $48 \div 6 = 8$," said David.

"But if we use your open number line, we can take away larger chunks instead. We start at 48 and take away 18 for 3 of the 6s and then take away 18 again. Then there are only 2 chunks of 6 left to take away to get to 0. We still get 8 bags." said David.

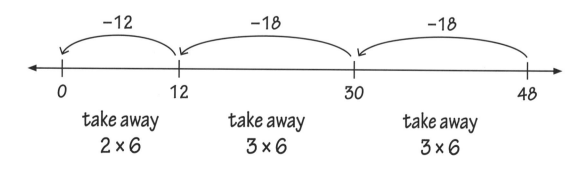

Solve-the-Problem Mini-Books: Multiplication & Division © Nancy Belkov, Scholastic Inc. (page 15)

"Dividing parts of 48 is faster than just taking away 6 at a time like on my number line," said Lucia.

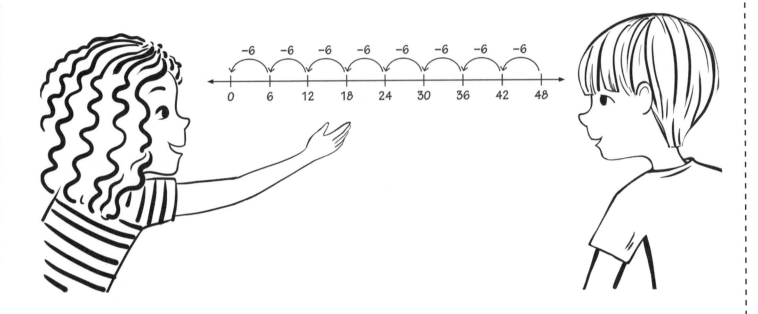

Your Turn

- How did Lucia and David use drawings to help them figure out how many bags they needed?

- How did Lucia and David use number lines to help them figure out how many bags they needed?

Solve-the-Problem Mini-Books: Multiplication & Division © Nancy Belkov, Scholastic Inc. (page 16)

Solve-the-Problem Mini-Books: Multiplication & Division © Nancy Belkov, Scholastic Inc. (page 17)

Name: _____

Finding the Quotient

Here are more problems. Try to solve each in at least two ways. Think about the strategies Lucia and David used.

1. Julio has 27 books to put on his shelves. He wants to put 9 books on each shelf. How many shelves does he need?

2. Nadia found 36 markers in her desk. She wanted to put them in 6 equal bundles held together with rubber bands. How many markers should she put in each bundle?

3. David had 25 special stickers to give out to 5 of his friends equally. How many stickers should he give to each friend?

4. Ritu had 21 special seashells to give to 7 of her friends equally. How many seashells should she give to each friend?

5. Ms. Thompson kept the class's writing materials in 6 containers. She tried to keep the same number of materials in each container. She had 54 new pencils. How many new pencils should she put in each of the containers?

Extension: Change the numbers in one of the problems above or create your own problem about dividing things into a certain number of groups. Solve your problem.

Solve-the-Problem Mini-Books: Multiplication & Division © Nancy Belkov, Scholastic Inc. (page 18)

Picture Frames

Solve-the-Problem Mini-Books: Multiplication & Division © Nancy Belkov, Scholastic Inc.

Think

- What is happening in this story?

- What do the students need to figure out?

- What is the important information?

Tariq and Maria are making 9 craft stick picture frames. Each frame uses 4 craft sticks and 8 craft buttons. Tariq and Maria need to figure out how many sticks and buttons they should buy.

1

Solve-the-Problem Mini-Books: Multiplication & Division © Nancy Belkov, Scholastic Inc. (page 19)

"I think it's 32. But I know a multiplication fact that will make this easier," said Maria.

"Good. I lost track skip counting. Now I'm not sure if it's 36 or 40 next!" said Tariq.

"It's easier to think about 10 picture frames instead of 9. I know that $10 \times 4 = 40$," said Maria.

"But we only want 9 picture frames. How can 10×4 help us?" asked Tariq.

3

"For 9 frames, we'll need 9 groups of 4 craft sticks and 9 groups of 8 craft buttons. Do you know how much 9 × 4 or 9 × 8 is?" Maria asked Tariq.

"I forget. I can skip count by 4 on this array of dots to find out. It has 9 rows of 4. I'll count 4, 8, 12, 16, 20, 24, 28. Hmmm, what's next?" said Tariq.

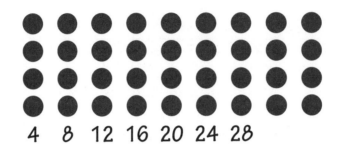

4   8   12   16   20   24   28

2

"Because 9 groups of 4 is almost as many as 10 groups of 4. Look, I drew 10 groups of 4 pretend craft sticks, or 40 sticks. That's one more group than we need, so I crossed out 1 group. 40 – 4 = 36, so 9 groups of 4 sticks must be 36 sticks," said Maria.

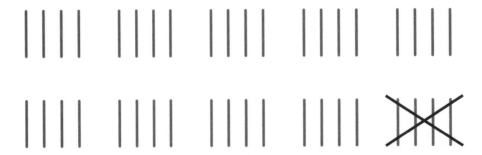

Start with 10 groups of 4 sticks
Then cross out 1 group of 4 sticks
10 × 4 = 40, so 9 × 4 = 36

4

Solve-the-Problem Mini-Books: Multiplication & Division © Nancy Belkov, Scholastic Inc. (page 20)

"That makes sense. I'll try your strategy to figure out 9 × 8 for our buttons. 10 × 8 = 80. If we remove one of the groups of 8 from 80, we get 72. So 9 groups of 8 is 72, like in my drawing," said Tariq.

10 groups of 8 buttons 10 × 8 = 80
Cross out 1 group of 8 buttons to have 9 groups
80 − 8 = 72, so 9 × 8 = 72

Solve-the-Problem Mini-Books: Multiplication & Division © Nancy Belkov, Scholastic Inc. (page 21)

"I agree. Each group of 8 is 2 groups of 4. 9 × 4 = 36. So if I add 36 + 36, I'll get the same answer I got when I started with 10 groups of 8 buttons. 9 × 8 = (9 × 4) + (9 × 4). It's still 72 buttons," said Tariq.

"Your picture is double my picture. I made groups of 4 for the sticks, and you made groups of 8 for the buttons. You have 2 × 4 in each of your groups. That's twice as many things in each group. So we can double 9 × 4 to get 9 × 8. I think that 9 × 8 = 2 × 9 × 4," said Maria.

6

Your Turn

- How did Tariq and Maria figure out the products for 9 × 4?

- How did Tariq and Maria figure out the product for 9 × 8?

- Why did Tariq and Maria double the product for 9 × 4 to find the product for 9 × 8?

- Do you have another strategy that helps you find products easily?

8

Name: _____

Finding Multiple Products

Here are more problems. Try to solve each in at least two ways. Think about the strategies Maria and Tariq used.

1. Polygon School's librarian planned to buy new books to give to 8 classrooms. She wanted to give each of the classrooms 4 science books and 8 fiction books. How many science books and how many fiction books did she need to buy?

2. Vincent exercised every day of the week. Each day, he ran around his block 3 times and jumped rope 6 times. How many times did he run around the block in one week? How many times did he jump rope in one week?

3. Purva and Jaidev wanted to fill 7 bags of food to donate to a food pantry. They wanted to put 4 cans of fruit and 8 cans of soup in each bag. How many cans of fruit and how many cans of soup did they need to fill the bags?

4. In Polygon School, fourth graders read to younger students 5 days a week. Each day, 5 fourth graders read to the kindergarten class, and 10 fourth graders read to the first-grade class. How many fourth graders read to the kindergartners each week? How many fourth graders read to the first graders each week?

Extension: Change the numbers in one of the problems above or create your own problem about finding the product of a certain number of groups with a certain amount in each group. Solve your problem.

Solve-the-Problem Mini-Books: Multiplication & Division © Nancy Belkov, Scholastic Inc. (page 24)

Basketballs for Each Class

The gym teacher, Ms. Parker, had 24 new basketballs and 32 old basketballs to give to 8 classrooms equally. She asked her students how many basketballs she should give to each class.

Solve-the-Problem Mini-Books: Multiplication & Division © Nancy Belkov, Scholastic Inc.

Think

- What is happening in this story?

- What do the students need to figure out?

- What is the important information?

1

Alex drew a diagram to figure out how to give out the new balls. "Ms. Parker can start by giving 2 new basketballs to each class. That's 2 x 8 which is 16 balls. Then she can give one more to each class. 16 + 8 = 24. So dividing all 24 new balls among 8 classrooms is 3 balls for each class. 3 × 8 = 24, so 24 ÷ 8 = 3," said Alex.

$$8 \times 2 = 16$$
$$8 \times 1 = 8$$
$$24 \div 8 = 3$$

Solve-the-Problem Mini-Books: Multiplication & Division © Nancy Belkov, Scholastic Inc. (page 25)

3

"I think Ms. Parker should give some of the new basketballs to each classroom and then give out the old basketballs," Alex said to Yi.

"Since the old basketballs are still good, I think she can put all of her basketballs together and give them to the classrooms," said Yi.

"Let's each find a way for Ms. Parker to give out the balls. Then we can compare our ideas," said Alex.

2

Then Alex figured out how to give out the 32 old balls. "Since 32 is more than 24, she can use 24 of the old balls and give 3 to each class. I already know that 24 ÷ 8 = 3. There would still be 8 more old balls to give out, 1 more for each class. So there would be 4 balls from last year for each class.

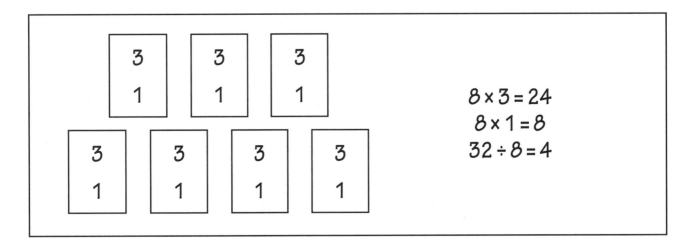

$$8 \times 3 = 24$$
$$8 \times 1 = 8$$
$$32 \div 8 = 4$$

4

Solve-the-Problem Mini-Books: Multiplication & Division © Nancy Belkov, Scholastic Inc. (page 26)

Alex showed his work to Yi and said that Ms. Parker should give 3 of the 24 new balls and 4 of the 32 old balls to each class.

"I got that too. She can give 7 balls to each classroom. Ms. Parker has 32 balls plus 24 balls. 32 + 24 = 56 balls to give out to 8 classrooms. So I divided 56 by 8. I kept taking away chunks of 8. Here is my work," said Yi.

56 – 8 = 48	First, I took away 8 balls
48 – 8 = 40	to give 1 ball to each class.
40 – 8 = 32	
32 – 8 = 24	I kept taking away 8 balls
24 – 8 = 16	to give 1 ball to each class.
16 – 8 = 8	
8 – 8 = 0	Altogether I did that 7 times.
	So 56 ÷ 8 = 7

"Great! We used different strategies and got the same answer each way we tried. I am glad all our classrooms can get 7 basketballs to use. We can share them and have fun!" said Yi.

"So you had to subtract balls 7 times to give out all 56 balls to the 8 classrooms. Let's try to subtract larger chunks to remove the balls in fewer steps. First, we subtract 24 balls to give 3 balls to each class, like this," said Alex.

$56 - 24 = 32$ $24 \div 8 = 3$ so take away three 8s and have 32 left

$32 - 24 = 8$ $24 \div 8 = 3$ so take away three more 8s and have 8 left

$8 - 8 = 0$ $8 \div 8 = 1$ so take away one more 8 and have 0 left

I took away seven 8s, so $56 \div 8 = 7$

Your Turn

- How did the diagram Alex made help him understand a way to give out the basketballs?

- How did Yi and Alex use subtraction and multiplication to help them figure out how to give out the basketballs?

Solve-the-Problem Mini-Books: Multiplication & Division © Nancy Belkov, Scholastic Inc. (page 28)

Name: _____

Finding the Amount in Each Group

Here are more problems. Try to solve each in at least two ways. Think about the strategies Yi and Alex used.

1. Ms. Thompson had 24 new boxes of markers and 8 old boxes of markers that were still in good condition. She wanted to spread the boxes out evenly among 4 work tables. How many boxes of markers should she put at each table?

2. At Polygon School, 30 fifth graders and 15 fourth graders volunteered to clean up the playground. The principal made 5 equal teams of volunteers to do the clean-up. How many students did the principal put on each team?

Solve-the-Problem Mini-Books: Multiplication & Division © Nancy Belkov, Scholastic Inc. (page 29)

3. Students at Polygon School were decorating 6 hallways with sparkly polygons. They had 30 sparkly pentagons and 24 sparkly octagons. The students wanted to put the same number of pentagons and octagons in each hallway. How many sparkly polygons will they have in each hallway when they are finished decorating?

4. Debra and Jamaal decided to make bracelets to sell at the school fair. They wanted to make 9 bracelets, each with the same number of beads. They had 45 beads. Then their mom gave them 27 new beads. How many beads could they put on each bracelet?

Extension: Change the numbers in one of the problems above or create your own problem about dividing things into a certain number of groups. Solve your problem.

Solve-the-Problem Mini-Books: Multiplication & Division © Nancy Belkov, Scholastic Inc. (page 30)

Bulletin Board Photos

- What is happening in this story?

- What do the students need to figure out?

- What is the important information?

Ms. Thompson asked Liam and Ashni to put 42 photos in an array on a bulletin board. She told them 7 photos would fit in a row and asked them how many photos they could put in each column to fit all 42 photos.

"Now I remember. A column stands up straight, and a row is horizontal. I think we need to figure out how many photos we will put on the board vertically, and still fit 42 photos. Let's keep making rows of 7 photos until we use all 42 photos. Then we'll see how many photos will be in each column," said Ashni.

"Ms. Thompson asked how many photos we should put in each column. What does she mean?" Ashni asked Liam.

"I made a sketch of 1 row of 7 photos. I know a row goes left to right like this, so I think a column goes up and down," said Liam.

"We could act it out like that. But I think it's easier to work with our sketch. I started a second row in the first column. If we finish that row, we'll have 2 × 7. I know 2 × 7 = 14, and that's a start. We can add 2 more rows to have 14 + 14," said Liam.

Solve-the-Problem Mini-Books: Multiplication & Division © Nancy Belkov, Scholastic Inc. (page 32)

"That gets us closer to using all 42 photos. We could also write equations to figure out how many chunks of 7 are in 42. That will help us see how many photos fit in each column," said Ashni.

$$2 \times 7 = 14$$
$$2 \times 7 = 14$$
$$2 \times 7 = 14$$

$$3 \times 14 = 42$$

Solve-the-Problem Mini-Books: Multiplication & Division © Nancy Belkov, Scholastic Inc. (page 33)

"Great! I know another fact that can help us remember how many chunks of 7 are in 42: $3 \times 7 = 21$. We could double that to see that 42 is 6×7. Let's go show Ms. Thompson our work!

	2 × 7
	2 × 7
	2 × 7

"I like how your equations show we need 2 rows of 7, then 2 more rows of 7, then 2 more rows of 7 to fit 42 photos on the board. That's 6 rows so we have 6 photos in each column, like this," said Liam.

Your Turn

- How did Ashni and Liam figure out how many 7s are in 42?

- How did their diagrams help them figure out how many photos could fit in each column?

- How could they use the fact 3 × 7 = 21 to figure out how many 7s are in 42?

Solve-the-Problem Mini-Books: Multiplication & Division © Nancy Belkov, Scholastic Inc. (page 34)

Name: _____

Finding the Number of Groups

Here are more problems. Try to solve each in at least two ways. Think about the strategies Liam and Ashni used.

1. Miguel's little brother used 21 blocks to make towers. He put 7 blocks in each tower. How many towers did he make?

2. Hana and Nikita made a chart for the class to keep track of attendance. They used the names of the 24 students in their class and put 8 names in each column. How many columns did they put in their chart?

3. Anna and Miki put 56 homemade muffins in boxes for a school bake sale. They put 7 muffins in each box. How many boxes did they fill?

4. Ms. Thompson's class set up 63 chairs for their guests to watch a class performance. They found that 9 chairs fit neatly in a row. How many rows did they set up?

Extension: Change the numbers in one of the problems above or create up your own division problem. Solve your problem.

Solve-the-Problem Mini-Books: Multiplication & Division © Nancy Belkov, Scholastic Inc. (page 36)

A Garden Fence

Ellie and Amir needed a fence around their garden. They knew the garden was 5 feet wide with an area of 35 square feet, but they needed to figure out its length.

Think

- What is happening in this story?

- What do the students need to figure out?

- What is the important information?

1

"Since we know it is 5 feet on one side, we can put 5 squares on that side. That's 5 square feet. We can keep putting columns of 5 in the garden picture. Then we can see how many chunks of 5 we can take away from 35 to figure out how long the other side is. So far, I drew 10 square feet," said Amir.

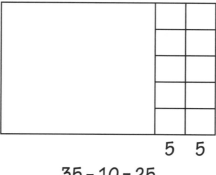

5   5

$35 - 10 = 25$

"So you are trying to figure out what times 5 equals 35. That's $35 \div 5$," said Ellie.

3

"Maybe a picture of our garden will help us. This shows it is 5 feet on one side," Ellie said to Amir.

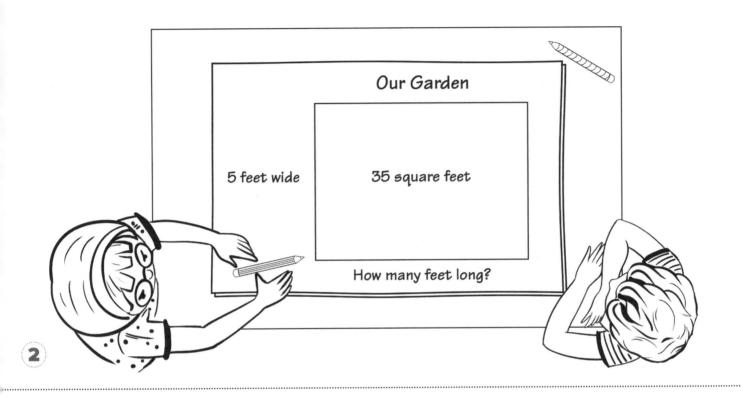

Our Garden

5 feet wide

35 square feet

How many feet long?

2

"Instead of drawing so many boxes, let's start at 35 on a number line and take away chunks of 5 until we get to 0, like this," said Ellie.

"That gives me another idea. We can take away fives from 35 in chunks. When you took away 2 groups of 5 from 35, you had 25 left. We can take away the whole chunk of 25 since we know that $5 \times 5 = 25$. So $25 \div 5 = 5$. We divide 25 by 5 and get 5," said Amir.

4

"I like the way you put together 2 × 5 = 10 and 5 × 5 = 25 to figure out how many groups of 5 are in 35. We can put them together in an open array to show that 5 chunks of 5 and 2 more chunks of 5 equal 25 plus 10, which is 35. Like this," said Ellie.

Our garden is 35 square feet

	5 feet	2 feet
5 feet wide	25 ÷ 5 = 5 square feet	10 ÷ 5 = 2 square feet

Solve-the-Problem Mini-Books: Multiplication & Division © Nancy Belkov, Scholastic Inc. (page 39)

"I think the people at the store will also want to know how many feet of fence we need altogether," said Ellie.

"They might. We can figure that out. Isn't it 7 + 7 + 5 + 5 , or 24 feet?" said Amir.

"Yes! That's the perimeter. Good thinking!" said Ellie.

"It's like we have 5 columns of 5 square units and 2 more columns of 5 square units. So the garden is 5 feet on one side and 7 feet on the other. Now I know we need fence pieces for 2 sides that are 5 feet and 2 sides that are 7 feet," said Amir.

Our garden is 35 square feet

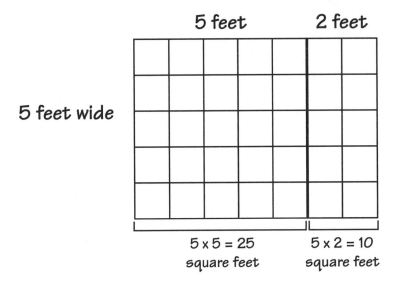

5 feet   2 feet

5 feet wide

5 x 5 = 25
square feet

5 x 2 = 10
square feet

Your Turn

- How did Amir and Ellie figure out how many fives are in 35?

- How did multiplication help them divide?

- How did knowing the area of the garden help them figure out the perimeter of the garden?

Solve-the-Problem Mini-Books: Multiplication & Division © Nancy Belkov, Scholastic Inc. (page 40)

Name: _____

Finding the Missing Side

Here are more problems. Try to solve each in at least two ways. Think about the strategies Amir and Ellie used.

1. Ms. Thompson taught her students how to knit. They knit rectangles that measured 24 square inches. The bottom of each rectangle was 8 inches. How tall did the students need to make each rectangle?

2. Tariq wanted a new rug for his bedroom. Each side of the new rug had to be less that 7 feet so that it could fit in his room. He liked a rug that had an area of 24 square feet. He knew it was 4 feet wide. Would that rug fit in his room?

Solve-the-Problem Mini-Books: Multiplication & Division © Nancy Belkov, Scholastic Inc. (page 41)

3. Students at Polygon School drew a plan for a picnic area. It had an area of 42 square meters. What are the missing measurements?

Polygon School Picnic Area

? meters

6 meters | 42 square meters | 6 meters

? meters

4. Here is a map of the library room at Polygon School. The area of the room is 72 square meters. What is the missing dimension?

Library Room

? meters

8 meters | 72 square meters | 8 meters

? meters

Extension: Create your own problem about a rectangular area. Tell the area and the length of the opposite sides. Do not tell the width of the other 2 opposite sides. Make a diagram of the space in your problem and solve your problem.

Solve-the-Problem Mini-Books: Multiplication & Division © Nancy Belkov, Scholastic Inc. (page 42)

A Terrier and a Great Dane

Ms. Thompson has two dogs, a terrier and a Great Dane. The terrier weighs 9 kilograms, and the Great Dane weighs 6 times as much. Ms. Thompson asked her students to figure out how much the Great Dane weighed.

Think

- What is happening in this story?

- What do the students need to figure out?

- What is the important information?

1

"I get it. If the Great Dane weighed 2 times as much as the 9-kilogram terrier, it would weigh 18 kilograms since $2 \times 9 = 18$. I can't draw weight, so I'll draw rectangles and pretend they each weigh 9 kilograms. That will help me think about the weight of the dogs," said Jung.

3

"What does Ms. Thompson mean when she says her Great Dane weighs 6 times as much as her terrier?" Jung asked Rosa.

"That's like what my mom means when she says I am 2 times as old as my sister," said Rosa.

"Hmmm. So how old is your sister and how old are you?" asked Jung.

"I am 8 and my sister is 4. So I am 2 times as old as her. 2 × 4 = 8," said Rosa.

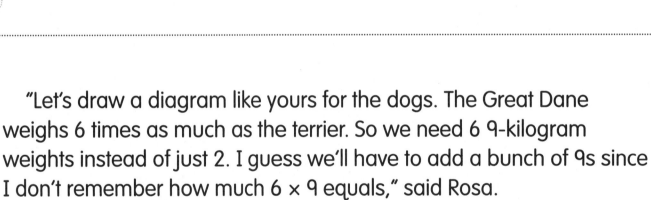

"Let's draw a diagram like yours for the dogs. The Great Dane weighs 6 times as much as the terrier. So we need 6 9-kilogram weights instead of just 2. I guess we'll have to add a bunch of 9s since I don't remember how much 6 × 9 equals," said Rosa.

"That's a lot of 9s to keep track of," said Jung.

Solve-the-Problem Mini-Books: Multiplication & Division © Nancy Belkov, Scholastic Inc. (page 44)

"Instead of adding chunks of 9, we can use 2 × 9 a bunch of times and add the groups of 18. Like in my diagram. So we add 36 + 18. Does that equal 54?" asked Jung.

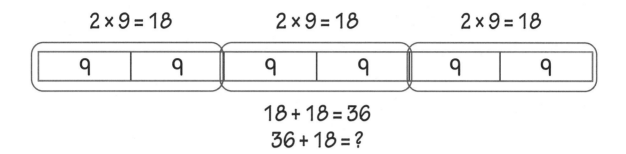

$$2 \times 9 = 18 \qquad 2 \times 9 = 18 \qquad 2 \times 9 = 18$$

| 9 | 9 | 9 | 9 | 9 | 9 |

$$18 + 18 = 36$$
$$36 + 18 = ?$$

"I think so. Let's check that with facts we know that are close to 6 × 9 like 5 × 9 and 6 × 10," said Rosa.

"You got 54 kilograms again. Let's check one more time. I always remember that 6 × 10 = 60, but that is 10 groups of 6 kilograms. That's too many chunks of 6. So we'll have to subtract a 6 to have 9 groups of 6 kilograms. 60 – 6 = 54. Since 9 × 6 = 54, 6 groups of 9 kilograms also equals 54. Now I'm sure the Great Dane must weigh 54 kilograms. We got the same answer 3 different ways," said Rosa.

$$6 + 6 + 6 + 6 + 6 + 6 + 6 + 6 + 6 + 6 = 60$$

$$10 \times 6 = 60$$
$$60 - 6 = 54$$
$$9 \times 6 = 54$$

Solve-the-Problem Mini-Books: Multiplication & Division © Nancy Belkov, Scholastic Inc. (page 45)

$$9 + 9 + 9 + 9 + 9 + 9 \qquad 5 \times 9 = 45$$
$$1 \times 9 = 9$$
$$45 + 9 = 54$$

"Good idea. I know that $5 \times 9 = 45$. When you multiply 5 by an even number, the product has 0 in the ones place. When you multiply 5 times an odd number, the product has 5 in the ones place. That helps me remember that $5 \times 8 = 40$ and $5 \times 9 = 45$. We just need one more 9 for 6×9," said Jung.

6

Your Turn

- How did Jung and Rosa use a picture to help them understand how to solve the problem?

- Jung and Rosa used different facts they know to find the product for 9×6. They used $2 \times 9 = 18$, $5 \times 9 = 45$, and $10 \times 6 = 60$. How did they use those facts to get 54 kilograms as their solution?

8

Solve-the-Problem Mini-Books: Multiplication & Division © Nancy Belkov, Scholastic Inc. (page 46)

Name: _____

Finding the Larger Amount

Here are more problems. Try to solve each in at least two ways. Think about the strategies Jung and Rosa used.

1. Rosa and her dad lifted weights together. Rosa lifted a 5-pound weight over her head. Her father lifted a weight that was 5 times as heavy. How heavy was the weight that Rosa's father lifted?

2. Jung practiced playing piano for 5 minutes on Monday. His mother said he should practice 6 times as many minutes on Tuesday. How many minutes did his mother want him to practice on Tuesday?

3. Jung figured out that his grandmother is 7 times as old as he is. Jung is 8 years old. How old is his grandmother?

Solve-the-Problem Mini-Books: Multiplication & Division © Nancy Belkov, Scholastic Inc. (page 47)

4. Rosa is 8 years old. Her uncle wouldn't tell her how old he is. He just said he is 6 times older than her. How old is Rosa's uncle?

5. Anya's great-grandfather is 9 times as old as she is. Anya is 9 years old. How old is her great-grandfather?

Extension: Change the numbers in one of the problems above or create your own problem about comparing two amounts when one amount is several times bigger than the other amount. Solve your problem.

Solve-the-Problem Mini-Books: Multiplication & Division © Nancy Belkov, Scholastic Inc. (page 48)

Buying Backpacks

Samira and Ronald shopped for backpacks with their dad and liked red ones that cost $49 each. Dad said those backpacks cost 7 times more than his backpack as a kid. Dad asked them to figure out how much his backpack had cost.

Think

- What is happening in this story?

- What do the students need to figure out?

- What is the important information?

1

"I don't know, but this might help. When I wanted to buy a fancy pen for $6, Mom said it was too expensive. She said it was 3 times as much as she would spend for one pen and that you could buy 3 good pens for the same price," said Samira.

$6 for a fancy pen = ☐ ☐ ☐

3

"I guess Dad thinks that the red backpacks are too expensive," Samira said to Ronald.

"Yes. He said they cost 7 times as much as his backpack cost when he was in school. What does he mean? How much did his backpack cost then?" asked Ronald.

"So your diagram shows that 1 fancy pen costs the same as 3 regular pens. Did the regular pens cost $2?" asked Ronald.

"Yes, because $6 ÷ 3 = $2. I know because $6 = 3 × $2," said Samira.

$6 for a fancy pen	=	$2 for 1 plain pen	$2 for 1 plain pen	$2 for 1 plain pen

Solve-the-Problem Mini-Books: Multiplication & Division © Nancy Belkov, Scholastic Inc. (page 50)

"I think we can multiply or divide to figure out how much Dad's old backpack cost," said Samira.

"We can draw a picture like yours to compare spending $49 on the red backpack to buying backpacks when Dad was our age," said Ronald.

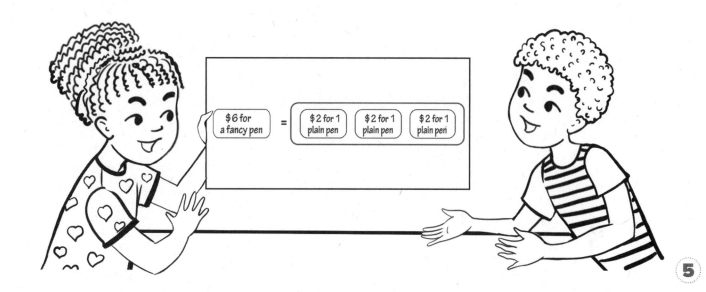

"Pretend Dad bought all 7 backpacks with $49. If those backpacks each cost $1, he'd spend $7. If they each cost $2, he'd spend $7 again. So I keep taking away $7 on my open number line until he spends $49, like this," said Samira.

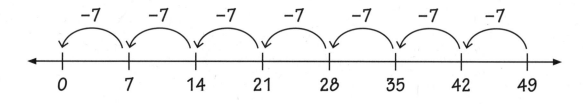

"I can also make $49 with facts I know: 5 x 7 = 35 and 2 x 7 = 14. That means 35 + 14 = 49. So Dad could buy the backpacks with $5 + $2. We get $7 for Dad's backpack both ways," said Ronald.

"The $49 backpack is 7 times as much as one of Dad's old backpacks. So 7 of those backpacks must have cost $49 altogether, and each one cost $49 ÷ 7," said Ronald.

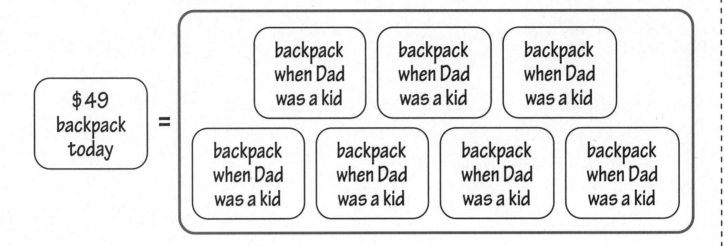

Your Turn

• How did thinking about pens help Ronald and Samira figure out how to try to solve this problem?

• How did Ronald and Samira figure out how many groups of $7 equal $49?

Solve-the-Problem Mini-Books: Multiplication & Division © Nancy Belkov, Scholastic Inc. (page 52)

Name: _____

Finding the Smaller Amount

Here are more problems. Try to solve each in at least two ways. Think about the strategies Samira and Ronald used.

1. Samira and Ronald's mom said that the hat Samira bought cost 3 times as much as Samira's mom spent on a hat when she was Samira's age. Samira's hat cost $27. How much did Samira's mom spend on her hat years ago?

2. Samira and Ronald's Aunt Mo said that she is 7 times older than her son Ben. Aunt Mo is 28 years old. How old is Ben?

Solve-the-Problem Mini-Books: Multiplication & Division © Nancy Belkov, Scholastic Inc. (page 53)

3. Samira and Ronald dug up potatoes at their uncle's farm and put them in a bag. Their uncle dug potatoes and put them in a different bag. Their uncle's bag weighed 54 pounds. His bag was 9 times heavier than Samira and Ronald's bag. How heavy was Samira and Ronald's bag?

4. Samira ran a mile on most sunny days over the summer. She ran a total of 63 miles. Her little sister ran with her a few of the days. Samira ran 7 times as many miles as her little sister. How many miles did her little sister run?

Extension: Change the numbers in one of the problems above or create your own problem about comparing amounts. Describe a situation where you know one amount and how many times larger it is than a smaller amount. Solve your problem.

Solve-the-Problem Mini-Books: Multiplication & Division © Nancy Belkov, Scholastic Inc. (page 54)

Lemonade for the Fair

Ms. Thompson's class is making lemonade with 64 ounces of lemon juice. Nicola and Hugo squeezed 8 ounces. Hugo thinks they still need to squeeze more than 2 times as much juice. Ms. Thompson asks them to figure out how many times as much juice they need to reach 64 ounces.

Solve-the-Problem Mini-Books: Multiplication & Division © Nancy Belkov, Scholastic Inc.

Think

- What is happening in this story?

- What do the students need to figure out?

- What is the important information?

1

"I get it. Wouldn't it look like this? With 8 more ounces we'll have 16 ounces. $2 \times 8 = 16$ or $16 \div 8 = 2$. So 16 ounces is 2 times as much as 8 ounces," said Nicola.

"Yes, but we need 64 ounces, not 16 ounces. We need to figure out how many times more than 8 ounces of lemon juice we need. We want to know __ $\times 8 = 64$ or how much $64 \div 8$ is," said Hugo.

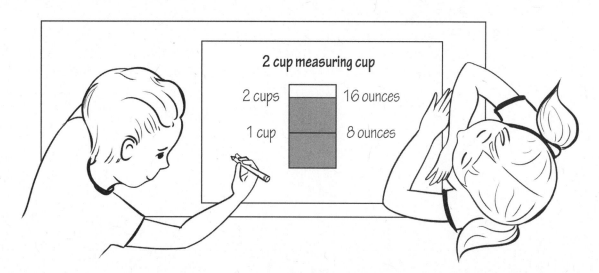

2 cup measuring cup

2 cups   16 ounces

1 cup   8 ounces

Solve-the-Problem Mini-Books: Multiplication & Division © Nancy Belkov, Scholastic Inc. (page 55)

3

"How do you know that we need more than 2 times as much lemon juice?" Nicola asked Hugo.

"I looked at our cup holding 8 ounces of juice and wondered what it would look like if we filled it to the 16-ounce mark," said Hugo.

②

"When I repeat my drawing, we have 2 sections of 8 ounces of juice, plus 2 more sections of 8 ounces of juice. That's 4 sections of 8 ounces. 16 + 16 = 32, so 4 × 8 = 32," said Nicola.

2-cup measuring cup	2-cup measuring cup
2 cups 16 ounces	2 cups 16 ounces
1 cup 8 ounces	1 cup 8 ounces

④

Solve-the-Problem Mini-Books: Multiplication & Division © Nancy Belkov, Scholastic Inc. (page 56)

"That's still not enough. 32 ounces of juice is 4 times as much as 8 ounces. If we draw that again, we'll have 64 ounces. So we need to squeeze 8 times as much juice as we have.
8 × 8 ounces = 64 ounces," said Hugo.

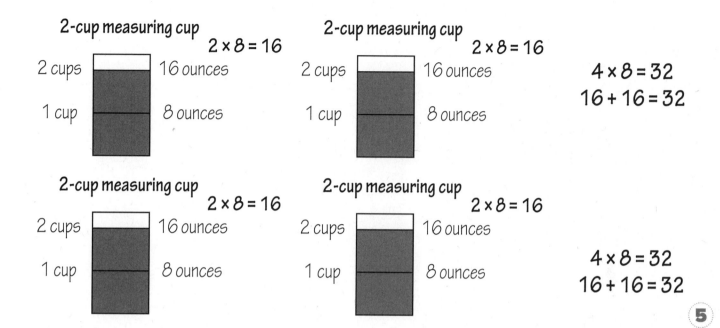

2-cup measuring cup
$2 \times 8 = 16$
2 cups   16 ounces
1 cup   8 ounces

2-cup measuring cup
$2 \times 8 = 16$
2 cups   16 ounces
1 cup   8 ounces

$4 \times 8 = 32$
$16 + 16 = 32$

2-cup measuring cup
$2 \times 8 = 16$
2 cups   16 ounces
1 cup   8 ounces

2-cup measuring cup
$2 \times 8 = 16$
2 cups   16 ounces
1 cup   8 ounces

$4 \times 8 = 32$
$16 + 16 = 32$

⑤

Solve-the-Problem Mini-Books: Multiplication & Division © Nancy Belkov, Scholastic Inc. (page 57)

"Great idea. You kept taking away 2 groups of 8 ounces, which is 16 ounces. You did that 4 times. So 64 ÷ 8 = 8. I think your number line will convince Ms. Thompson that we need more help to squeeze enough lemons!" said Hugo.

⑦

"Then we definitely need help to get to 64 ounces! Here's an open number line to show that we need to squeeze 8 times as much juice as we already have. I took away jumps of 2 times as much juice as we already made. Let's show this to Ms. Thompson and ask her to find some students to help us," said Nicola.

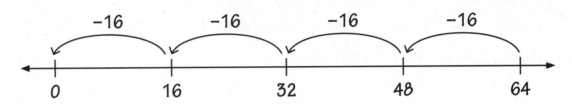

I keep taking away 2 × 8.

−16   −16   −16   −16

0   16   32   48   64

6

Your Turn

• Why did Hugo think 64 ounces was a lot of lemon juice in the beginning of the story?

• How did Hugo and Nicola use pictures and a number line to help them solve the problem?

8

Name: _____

Comparing Quantities

Here are more problems. Try to solve each in at least two ways. Think about the strategies Nicola and Hugo used.

1. One year the fair was on a very hot day, and the third graders sold 45 cups of lemonade. Ms. Thompson said that another year the fair was on a cold, rainy day, and the third graders only sold 9 cups of lemonade. How many times more lemonade was sold on the sunny day than on the rainy day?

2. Marco waters the vegetables in his garden when they seem to be dry. Monday was a sunny day, and Marco used 35 liters of water to water his vegetable garden. On Saturday he used 7 liters of water to water his vegetable garden. How many times more water did Marco use on Monday than on Saturday?

3. Tomás's bus drives 36 blocks to get to school. His sister's school is closer to their home. Her bus drives 9 blocks to get to school. How many times farther does Tomás's bus drive to get to school?

4. Lisa and Jerome bought a new jump rope. It was folded up in a package and measured 9 inches long. They unfolded it, and the jump rope was 81 inches long. How many times longer was the jump rope when they unfolded it?

Extension: Change the numbers in one of the problems above or create your own problem about comparing amounts. Describe a situation in which you want to figure out how many times larger or smaller one amount is compared to another. Solve your problem.

Solve-the-Problem Mini-Books: Multiplication & Division © Nancy Belkov, Scholastic Inc. (page 60)

School Mural

Jabari and Chloe told their grandfather about a project at their school. Students were painting tiles of 1 foot by 1 foot for a mural that would be 6 feet high by 50 feet long. Their grandfather asked them to figure out how many square feet the mural would cover.

Solve-the-Problem Mini-Books: Multiplication & Division © Nancy Belkov, Scholastic Inc.

Think

- What is happening in this story?

- What do the students need to figure out?

- What is the important information?

1

Our School Mural

6 feet

50 feet

"So is each of your little squares supposed to be one of our painted tiles?" asked Chloe.

"Yes, and each column will be 6 feet high," said Jabari.

"And the bottom number says the mural is 50 feet long. Does that mean that the art teacher will put up 50 columns of tiles?" asked Chloe.

Solve-the-Problem Mini-Books: Multiplication & Division © Nancy Belkov, Scholastic Inc. (page 61)

3

"What did Grandpa mean about how many square feet?" Chloe asked Jabari.

"Our paper tiles will be 1 foot by 1 foot. That means the tile will be 1 square foot. When the art teacher arranges them on the wall, the squares will fill a space like this," said Jabari.

Our School Mural

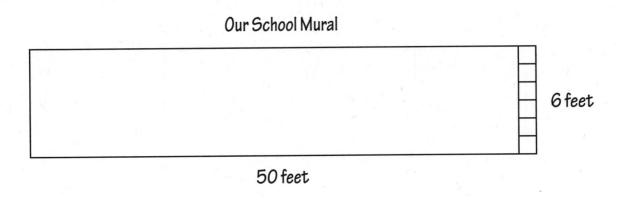

6 feet

50 feet

"I guess so. Each column will be 1 foot wide and 6 feet high. Grandpa asked us how many square feet the mural will measure. He wants to know the area of the mural, which is the same as saying the number of 1 foot by 1 foot squares that fit in the mural," said Jabari.

"How do we figure out the number of square feet? Do we have to make columns of 6 boxes all the way across and count all of them?" asked Chloe.

Solve-the-Problem Mini-Books: Multiplication & Division © Nancy Belkov, Scholastic Inc. (page 62)

6 rows of 5 groups of 10

10 tiles	10 tiles	10 tiles	10 tiles	10 tiles
10 tiles	10 tiles	10 tiles	10 tiles	10 tiles
10 tiles	10 tiles	10 tiles	10 tiles	10 tiles
10 tiles	10 tiles	10 tiles	10 tiles	10 tiles
10 tiles	10 tiles	10 tiles	10 tiles	10 tiles
10 tiles	10 tiles	10 tiles	10 tiles	10 tiles

6×5 groups of 10
6×50

"We could, but 50 columns of 6 tiles is a lot to draw. That's 50×6 or 6×50. What if we draw groups of 10 tiles to fill each row of 50, like this?" said Jabari.

"Why do you think that is true?" asked Chloe.

"Because 50 is 5 tens or 5×10, so $6 \times 50 = 6 \times 5$ tens, just like in your picture. You have 6 rows of 5 groups of 10. See what I mean?" asked Jabari.

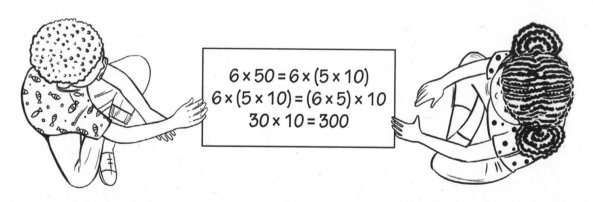

$$6 \times 50 = 6 \times (5 \times 10)$$
$$6 \times (5 \times 10) = (6 \times 5) \times 10$$
$$30 \times 10 = 300$$

"I get it. We multiply 6×5 and get 30. We have 30 groups of 10. 3 tens are 30, but 30 tens are 300. So the mural will be 300 square feet. Let's go tell Grandpa," said Chloe.

Solve-the-Problem Mini-Books: Multiplication & Division © Nancy Belkov, Scholastic Inc. (page 63)

"Great. Then we can count by tens. We need to draw 6 rows with 5 groups of 10 in each row. I'll pretend we put 10 tiles in each group. When I count, I get to 300. So the area is 300 square feet," said Chloe.

1st row	10	20	30	40	50
2nd row	60	70	80	90	100
3rd row	110	120	130	140	150
4th row	160	170	180	190	200
5th row	210	220	230	240	250
6th row	260	270	280	290	300

"I think that's right. I also think we can just multiply 6 × 5 to get 30. Then we'll see that there will be 30 groups of 10 which is 300," said Jabari.

6

Your Turn

• How did Jabari help Chloe understand how to find the area?

• What strategies did Chloe and Jabari use to multiply 6 × 50?

8

Solve-the-Problem Mini-Books: Multiplication & Division © Nancy Belkov, Scholastic Inc. (page 64)

Name: _____

Using Multiples of 10 to Find Area

Here are more problems. Try to solve each in at least two ways. Think about the strategies Chloe and Jabari used.

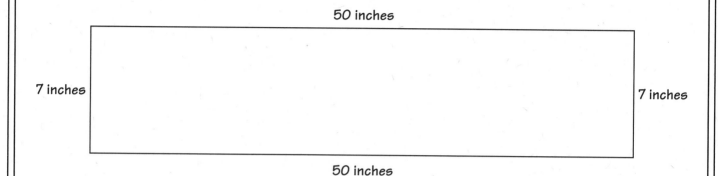

1. Chloe and Jabari have a little brother named Claude. He made a long building out of blocks. Jabari drew this diagram to show the measurements of Claude's building. Use the diagram to find the area of Claude's building.

2. The parents at Polygon School are planning to make a path to the school's playground. The path will measure 6 feet by 80 feet. What will be the area of the new path?

Solve-the-Problem Mini-Books: Multiplication & Division © Nancy Belkov, Scholastic Inc. (page 65)

3. Yi is figuring out where her bookcase will fit in her room. The bottom of the bookcase is a rectangle that measures 8 inches by 40 inches. What is the area of the bottom of the bookcase?

4. Sonali is knitting a scarf for her brother. The scarf is 8 inches wide. She wants the scarf to be 70 inches long. What will be the area of the scarf when she is finished?

Extension: Change the numbers in one of the problems above or create your own problem where you need to find the product of a single-digit number and a multiple of 10. Solve your problem.

Solve-the-Problem Mini-Books: Multiplication & Division © Nancy Belkov, Scholastic Inc. (page 66)

Writing Letters

Ms. Thompson's class needs enough envelopes to write 125 letters to pen pals. They have 7 boxes of envelopes. Each box has 30 envelopes. Ms. Thompson asked her students to figure out how many envelopes they would have left over.

Think

• What is happening in this story?

• What do the students need to figure out?

• What is the important information?

1

"Because we have 3 groups of 10 envelopes in one box, and I imagined 4 of those boxes," said Reina.

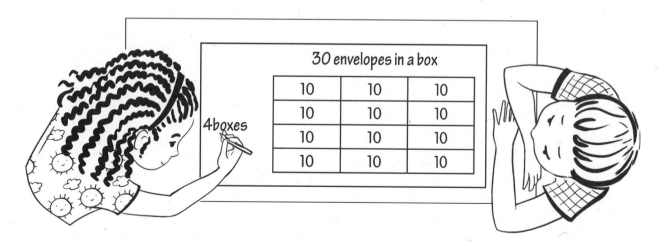

"I get it. Each of the 4 rows in your array has 3 groups of 10. That's 4 × 3 × 10. 4 × 3 = 12, so we'd have 12 tens. That's 120. Almost 125. That means we have more than enough in 7 boxes," said Sam.

3

"Are you sure we have enough envelopes for 125 letters?" Sam asked Reina.

"I'm sure we do. We'd almost have enough envelopes if we only had 4 boxes of 30 envelopes," said Reina.

"Why do you think that?" asked Sam.

"But Ms. Thompson asked how many extra envelopes we would have. Do you have an idea about how to figure that out?" asked Reina.

"I think we need to know exactly how many envelopes we have altogether. Let's start with an open array of 4 groups of 30 envelopes. It would be sort of like yours, but without all the groups of 10. I'll put on a section showing 3 more boxes of 30 envelopes to show all 7 boxes," said Sam.

4 boxes	30 envelopes in a box
	4 x 30 envelopes = 120 envelopes
3 boxes	3 x 30 envelopes = 90 envelopes

Solve-the-Problem Mini-Books: Multiplication & Division © Nancy Belkov, Scholastic Inc. (page 68)

"Great! You split up 7 boxes into 4 boxes and 3 boxes to make smaller arrays inside the big array. That breaks a harder problem into easier problems. So 7 × 30 = (4 + 3) × 30. That's (4 × 30) + (3 × 30). We know 4 × 30 = 120. I also know 3 × 3 = 9, so 3 × 30 = 9 tens or 90. That makes 120 + 90 envelopes," said Reina.

"I agree! That's 210 envelopes. 120 + 80 = 200, so 120 + 90 = 210. Now how many extra envelopes will we have after we use 125 of the 210 envelopes?" asked Sam.

30 envelopes in a box

4 boxes	4 × 30 envelopes = 120 envelopes
3 boxes	3 × 30 envelopes = 90 envelopes

"I also got 85 extra envelopes by adding up from 125 to 210 on a number line," said Reina.

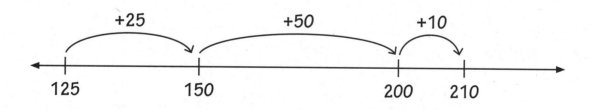

"So we'll have extra envelopes left over. That's good news!" said Sam.

Solve-the-Problem Mini-Books: Multiplication & Division © Nancy Belkov, Scholastic Inc. (page 69)

"Let's both figure that out and compare our answers. I'll add up on an open number line to find the answer," said Reina.

"Okay. I can easily subtract 10 and 75 from 210 to get to 125. Then I add 10 and 75 together for the extra envelopes. Like this," said Sam.

$$210 - 10 = 200$$
$$200 - 75 = 125$$
$$10 + 75 = 85 \text{ extra envelopes}$$

Your Turn

- How did Sam and Reina use arrays to figure out how many envelopes they needed for the pen pal letters, and how many extras they would have?

- What are the steps Sam and Reina used to answer Ms. Thompson's question?

Solve-the-Problem Mini-Books: Multiplication & Division © Nancy Belkov, Scholastic Inc. (page 70)

Name: _____

Using Multiple Operations

Here are more problems. Try to solve each in at least two ways. Think about the strategies Sam and Reina used.

1. Polygon School received 9 boxes of paper. Each box weighed 40 pounds. The school also received 3 boxes of desk equipment. Each of those boxes weighed 70 pounds. How many pounds did these boxes weigh altogether?

2. Polygon School has 24 boxes of pencils for the third-grade classes. There are 4 third-grade classes, and each class will receive the same number of pencil boxes. Each box has 50 pencils in it. How many pencils will each class receive?

3. Debra and Martin brought ribbon to school for an art project. Debra brought 5 rolls of ribbon, and each roll was 90 centimeters long. Martin brought 7 rolls of ribbon, and each of his rolls was 70 centimeters long. Who brought more ribbon to school? How much more ribbon did that person bring?

4. There were 8 classes in the school chorus. Each of the 8 classes had 60 guests coming to a performance in the auditorium. There were 515 seats in the auditorium. How many seats did the guests fill? How many seats were leftover?

Extension: Change the numbers in one of the problems above or create your own problem where you need to find the product of a single-digit number and a multiple of 10. Consider creating a problem that also requires adding or subtracting to figure out the answer. Solve your problem.

Solve-the-Problem Mini-Books: Multiplication & Division © Nancy Belkov, Scholastic Inc. (page 72)

Running Tracks at Polygon School

Ms. Thompson posed this problem: "We need to design 3 trails in the shapes of a regular pentagon, a square, and an equilateral triangle. The total length of the trails is between 900 and 1,000 meters. What are the dimensions of the shapes?"

Miki said that the pentagon sides could measure 90 meters each and the sides of the other trails could be 70 meters each. Ms. Thompson asked the class if those dimensions work.

Think
- What is happening in this story?
- What do the students need to figure out?
- What is the important information?

1

"Great. Let's also write the side lengths that Miki suggested next to the sides. We have to figure out how many meters you would run if you ran around all of our polygon trails," said Rahul.

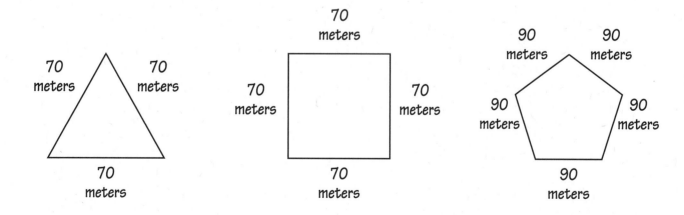

3

"That is a lot to think about. How can we get started?" Rahul asked Darcy.

"I drew the polygons to help us think about what to do next," said Darcy.

"But isn't that just finding the perimeter of the shapes? Should we add all those sides together?" asked Darcy.

"That would work. But adding three 3 groups of 70 + 4 groups of 70 + 5 groups of 90 is a lot of numbers to keep track of," said Rahul.

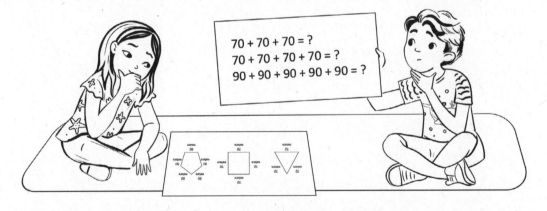

70 + 70 + 70 = ?
70 + 70 + 70 + 70 = ?
90 + 90 + 90 + 90 + 90 = ?

"Let's do one polygon at a time instead. Then we can add the perimeters of the polygons together," said Rahul.

Solve-the-Problem Mini-Books: Multiplication & Division © Nancy Belkov, Scholastic Inc. (page 74)

"Yes, and let's multiply the lengths of the sides. It will be quicker and easier. The perimeter of the triangle is 3 × 70, the perimeter of the square is 4 × 70, and the perimeter of the pentagon is 5 × 90," said Darcy.

"Yes, that's right. And I know that 3 × 7 = 21. So 3 × 70 is 21 tens or 210," said Rahul.

"Since 3 × 70 equals 210, we just add one more 70 for 4 × 70. That means 4 × 70 = 280," said Darcy.

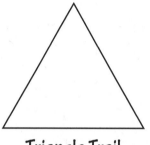

Triangle Trail
Perimeter = 210 meters

Square Trail
Perimeter = 280 meters

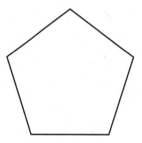

Pentagon Trail

"Let's read the problem again. It says we need to figure out if those measurements would total between 900 and 1,000 meters," said Darcy.

"Good reminder. I think Miki's solution works. 280 + 210 is almost 500. 500 + 450 is more than 900 since 500 + 400 = 900," said Rahul.

"Yes, and it's less than 1,000. Let's tell Ms. Thompson that the side measurements will work," said Darcy.

Solve-the-Problem Mini-Books: Multiplication & Division © Nancy Belkov, Scholastic Inc. (page 75)

"Now let's work on the pentagon. The sides of Pentagon Trail are 90, not 70," said Rahul.

"We can skip count by 5s to get 5 × 9," said Darcy.

"Sometimes I multiply by 10 when one of the factors is 9. I know 5 × 10 = 50. But we only have 9 groups of 5, so we subtract a 5. 50 – 5 = 45. So here are all of our perimeters," said Rahul.

"Now that we know all the perimeters, are we done?" asked Rahul.

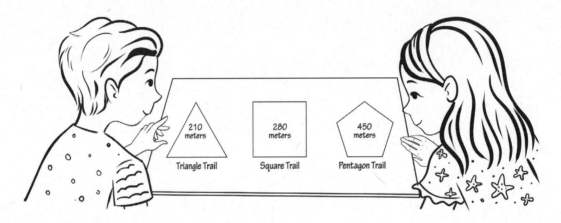

210 meters — Triangle Trail   280 meters — Square Trail   450 meters — Pentagon Trail

6

Your Turn

- How did Rahul and Darcy start solving this problem?

- What did Rahul and Darcy do to be sure to solve all the parts of the problem?

8

Name: _____

Multiplying to Find Perimeter

Here are more problems. Try to solve each in at least two ways. Think about the strategies Rahul and Darcy used.

1. Qian wants to design a trail in the shape of a regular pentagon. He wants each side to measure 70 meters. What will be the total length of his trail?

2. Gloria thought the school should have a regular octagon for a running trail. She wanted the total length of the trail to be less than 500 meters. Can her trail have sides that measure 60 meters and still total less than 500 meters? Show how you know.

3. Omar and Ana are designing a trail shaped like a regular hexagon. The total length needs to be less than 600 meters. The length of each side should be a multiple of 10. What is the largest perimeter their trail could be?

4. Some students in Ms. Thompson's class want to have a regular hexagon and a regular octagon for their trails. They want the side lengths to be between 50 and 100 meters. The combined length of the two trails should be between 900 and 1,000 meters. What side lengths could the hexagon and octagon have? Is there more than one solution for this problem?

Extension: Change the numbers in one of the problems above or make your own problem where you need to find the product of a single-digit number and a multiple of 10. Consider making a problem that also requires adding or subtracting to figure out the answer. Solve your problem.

Solve-the-Problem Mini-Books: Multiplication & Division © Nancy Belkov, Scholastic Inc. (page 78)

Answer Key

Title	Answers	Problem-solving strategies include:
Writing Story Problems (Writing Word Problems), *pp. 11–12*	Story problems will vary. Check student work. **1.** 40 **2.** 8 **3.** 7 **4.** 45	• Use repeated addition or subtraction • Skip count • Draw an array using given factors or given total • Use known multiplication facts to multiply with related factors • Divide by multiplying up • Use multiplication to solve division situations • Add up or subtract back in chunks of given group or number of groups
Greeting Cards (Finding the Quotient), *pp. 17–18*	**1.** 3 shelves **2.** 6 markers **3.** 5 stickers **4.** 3 seashells **5.** 9 pencils	• Draw a diagram to repeat given amount to reach given total • Divide by multiplying up • Use known multiplication facts to multiply with related factors • Divide by partial quotients • Use repeated addition or subtraction • Add up in chunks of given group
Picture Frames (Finding Multiple Products), *pp. 23–24*	**1.** 32 science books, 64 fiction books **2.** 21 times running, 42 times jumping rope **3.** 28 cans of fruit, 56 cans of soup **4.** 25 readers to kindergarten, 50 readers to first grade	• Draw an array or diagram using given factors • Skip count • Use known multiplication facts to multiply with related factors, such as doubles
Basketballs for Each Class (Finding the Amount in Each Group), *pp. 29–30*	**1.** 8 boxes **2.** 9 students **3.** 9 polygons **4.** 8 beads	• Draw a diagram showing given number of groups, and distribute items equally to reach given total • Divide by multiplying up • Use known multiplication facts to multiply with related factors • Divide by partial quotients • Add up or subtract back in chunks using given number of groups
Bulletin Board Photos (Finding the Number of Groups), *pp. 35–36*	**1.** 3 towers **2.** 3 columns **3.** 8 boxes **4.** 7 rows	• Draw an array using given factor to reach given total • Divide by multiplying up • Use known multiplication facts to multiply with related factors • Use repeated addition • Add up in chunks of given group

A Garden Fence (Finding the Missing Side), *pp. 41–42*	**1.** 3 inches **2.** Yes **3.** 7 meters **4.** 9 meters	• Use repeated addition or subtraction • Draw an array using given factor and given total • Add up or subtract back in chunks of given group • Use known multiplication facts to multiply with related factors • Divide by partial quotients
A Terrier and a Great Dane (Finding the Larger Amount), *pp. 47–48*	**1.** 25 pounds **2.** 30 minutes **3.** 56 years old **4.** 48 years old **5.** 81 years old	• Draw a diagram of a given number of groups, a given number of times • Use known multiplication facts to multiply with related factors • Add up or subtract back in chunks of given group
Buying Backpacks (Finding the Smaller Amount), *pp. 53–54*	**1.** $9 **2.** 4 years old **3.** 6 pounds **4.** 9 miles	• Draw a diagram of a given number of groups and fill groups to reach the larger amount • Use repeated subtraction • Use known multiplication facts to divide • Add up or subtract back in chunks of given group • Divide by partial quotients
Lemonade for the Fair (Comparing Quantities), *pp. 59–60*	**1.** 5 times more lemonade **2.** 5 times more water **3.** 4 times farther **4.** 9 times longer	• Draw a diagram of a smaller group and repeat to reach a larger amount • Add up or subtract back in chunks of given group • Use known multiplication facts to divide
School Mural (Using Multiples of 10 to Find Area), *pp. 65–66*	**1.** 350 square inches **2.** 480 square feet **3.** 320 square inches **4.** 560 square inches	• Draw an array using a given factor in chunks of 10 and a given total • Add up in chunks using multiples of 10 • Use single-digit multiplication facts to multiply by a multiple of 10 • Skip count by tens • Use the associative property
Writing Letters (Using Multiple Operations), *pp. 71–72*	**1.** 570 pounds **2.** 300 pencils **3.** Martin brought 40 centimeters more **4.** 480 seats were filled and 35 were leftover	• Draw an array using given multiple of tens factor in chunks of 10 • Add up in chunks using multiples of 10 • Use single-digit multiplication facts to multiply by a multiple of 10 • Use partial products to find the total • Use the associative property
Running Tracks at Polygon School (Multiplying to Find Perimeter), *pp. 77–78*	**1.** 350 meters **2.** Yes **3.** 540 meters **4.** Answers will vary.	• Draw diagrams to show repeated amounts • Use known multiplication facts to multiply with related factors • Use single-digit multiplication facts to multiply by a multiple of 10